I HEARD YOU

How To Achieve What You Want and Live Happy!

Marc Walker

© Copyright 2019 by Marc Walker

All rights reserved.

The reproduction, transmission, and duplication of any of the content found herein, including any specific or extended information, will be done as an illegal act regardless of the end form the information ultimately takes. This includes copied versions of the work both physical, digital and audio unless express consent of the Publisher is provided beforehand. Any additional rights reserved.

Furthermore, the information that can be found within the pages described forthwith shall be considered both accurate and truthful when it comes to the recounting of facts. As such, any use, correct or incorrect, of the provided information will render the Publisher free of responsibility as to the actions taken outside of their direct purview. Regardless, there are zero scenarios where the original author or the Publisher can be deemed liable in any fashion for any damages or hardships that may result from any of the information discussed herein.

This is a legally binding declaration that is considered both valid and fair by both the Committee of Publishers Association and the American Bar Association and should be considered as legally binding within the United States.

Dedication

To my parents, who taught me to hear …

and then take action to achieve all my goals!

Table of Contents

Introduction	11
Chapter 1: The Difference Between Hearing and Listening Carefully	17
Chapter 2: Learn From Those Who Have Already Achieved Your Goal	23
How Do You Pick Your Mentor?	24
What Do You Do With Your Mentor?	28
Chapter 3: Why You Are Where You Are Now and not Where You Would Like To Be	31
The Most Important Question: Why Aren't You There Yet?	33
How To Take Responsibility For Where You Are Right Now	36
What Do You Do With Your Responsibility?	39
Chapter 4: After Heard, Take Action	45
Why You Are not Immediately Jumping Into Action	46
Understanding the Lifecycle Of Habits and Changing Habits	50
How To Actually Implement What Your Mentor Has Taught You	54
Chapter 5	58
Define Your Goals	58
Why You Need To Have Goals	59

Using Your Findings To Create Your Goals — 62
Ensuring Your Goals Align With Your Bigger Picture — 65

Chapter 6: The Characteristics Of a Successful Goal — 70

What Should a Goal Be In Order To Be Successful? — 71
A Successful Goal Needs To Be Specific — 74
A Successful Goal Needs To Be Measurable — 77
A Successful Goal Needs To Be Credible — 79
A Successful Goal Needs To Be Motivating — 82

Chapter 7: A Specific Goal — 86

Defining the Goal, You Are Achieving — 88
Getting Intimate With the Specific Details Of That Goal — 90
Summarizing Your Specific Goal — 94

Chapter 8: A Measurable Goal — 97

Using Your Specifics To Define Your Measurements — 101
Identifying Your Goal's Milestones — 103
Adapting Your Milestones To Your Personal Needs — 108

Chapter 9: A Credible Goal — 111

Creating Goals That Are Realistic — 112
Getting Clear On Why You Care — 114

Aligning Your Goal and Action Steps
  With Your Bigger Picture 117
Chapter 10: A Motivating Goal 121
  Identifying the Motivational Parts Of
  Your Goal 123
  Infusing Your Goal With Motivational
  Qualities 125
Chapter 11: The Importance Of Chunking Down 129
  Eating the Elephant One Bite at a Time 131
  Chunking Your Goal Down Into Action
  Steps For Your To-Do List 134
Chapter 12: The Importance Of Acquiring a Method 137
  Turning Back To Your Mentor 139
  Implementing the Methods Your Mentors
  Use 143
Chapter 13: Kill Your Fears 149
  What Are Fears, Really? 150
  How To Reframe Your Fears 151
  Developing the Confidence To Succeed 153
Chapter 14: Dream It Vividly Every Day 157
  The Value Of Visualization 158
  How You Can Turn Your Goal Into a
  Visualization Practice 160
  Turning Your Visualization Practice Into
  a Daily Habit 163
Conclusion 169

Introduction

Achieving what you want in life and living a life that truly makes you happy is something that we all deserve to experience, and it is something that every single one of us has the power of achieving in our lives. If you have been looking around at your life and realizing that certain circumstances do not add up to you achieving what you want, or you experiencing deep unhappiness in your life, then chances are you are ready to make a change. You are ready to see yourself transform this area of your life and turn it into something magnificent, and something you can be proud of. Something that will genuinely make you happy.

Having that desire to make a change in your life is powerful, and it truly is at the root of everything you want in this lifetime.

However, having that desire alone is not enough to get you to the point where you actually experience change in your life and start living a life that makes you truly happy. That desire alone is merely a dream that you can talk about religiously and share with your family and friends over and over. For many, that dream even becomes a point of shame as they begin to acknowledge that, no, they still have not achieved it, and they are not even on track for doing so. It is not unusual for people to spend years of their lives, explaining why things have not changed for them yet, and why it seems like nothing will ever change. Some people even use humor as a way to offset the fact that nothing is changing by joking about how they are still in the same old job, or they are still single or still carrying around the extra weight or unhealthy lifestyle because they have not made a change yet. The sad thing is, most of these people genuinely believe that some uncontrollable circumstance in their lives is responsible for why they are still experiencing the same misfortune that they have been complaining about for so long. They truly believe that there is nothing they can do and so they consistently sit back and complain, joke, and blame everyone and everything else for why they are still in the same unfortunate circumstances year after year.

Of course, this is not true. The reality is that every single one of us has the power within to decide that we are done complaining, joking, and blaming, and we are ready to experience an *actual* change in our lives. We individually have more power than we think, and that power can effortlessly be tapped into and used to create overnight changes in our lives, even when we think change is impossible. We have seen it happen time and again: people completely transforming their lives by changing the way they view and use money, or changing the way they view and participate in their love lives. We see people transform their relationships, their careers, their health, and virtually every other aspect of their lives. And, if we are not yet ready to accept that we have this power too, we blame their success on them having some form of magical power to suddenly create such a significant change in their lives. The reality is, though, they do not have any form of magical power. The people who change their lives and experience something so magnificent that people call it magic are no different than you are, which means that there is absolutely no reason why you, too, cannot tap into this "magical" transformation.

The only thing you need to do to take yourself out of this victim mindset and raise yourself into the life you desire is to learn how to listen and how to act. That's right: the minute you stop *hearing* about how change works and start actually *listening to* what people are telling you and *acting on* what you have learned is the minute change starts. As soon as that change starts, it will develop a momentum that is almost unstoppable as you begin rapidly ending old self-limiting behaviors and mindsets and instead stepping into a reality of growth and change. Before you know it, you too will be living a life that you love, and that genuinely makes you happy. Plus, you will realize that you have the power to uplift yourself into even more success and happiness, meaning that there is truly no limitation or ceiling on how far you can go.

It's time for you to learn about this essential element of change and to stop blaming the people who have changed before you for trying to sell you snake oil whenever you reach out for support in changing your ways. You need to start taking responsibility for yourself and for your results and start actually making the necessary change today so that you can begin living the life you truly want, and the life that makes you truly happy. Are you ready? Let's begin.

Chapter 1

The Difference Between Hearing and Listening Carefully

It is safe to say that every single one of us has something in our lives that we wish to improve on. It is human nature to want to change areas of our lives so that they better reflect what truly want for ourselves, whether that be better finances, better health, a better career, or any other number of things that could truly improve the quality of your life. Unfortunately, what most people do not realize is that improving the quality of your life cannot be done simply by *hearing* about what needs to happen. It is accomplished by *listening* to what needs to happen, and then actually

17

implementing the changes that you have heard. Many people who claim they are ready to make a change in their lives will go ahead and attend seminars or weekend classes in an effort to learn more and, while they will learn more, they never actually implement what they have learned. Instead, they feel satisfied that they have made an effort, and then they revert back to blaming everything and everyone else for why no actual changes have been made. In reality, the bigger problem is not the circumstances of this person's life but their unwillingness to actually listen to and implement the changes that need to take place in order for them to create the life they want.

It is important to understand that people who attend these seminars and go into the idea of change with great intentions only to fall short of making any actual change are not bad people. Instead, they are people who are ultimately misguided on what it will take to make actual changes in their lives and so they have found themselves repeatedly falling short of achieving their goals. You may realize this to be true by looking at yourself and your own efforts to change your life, especially if you realize that despite how much you "know" you have never actually implemented most of what you have learned. In this case, you may be feeling like you are running an uphill marathon in that you find yourself constantly struggling with the process of actually implementing what you have learned. Fortunately, there is plenty that can be done to help you step away from simply hearing about what needs to happen and actually listening to what can be done to help you make lasting changes in your life.

One of the biggest keys to making true changes in your life is to recognize that you want change to happen in the first place, and then to become willing to do whatever it takes to make that change happen. This means that you need to stop thinking that showing up is enough and start doing everything you can to absorb as much as possible out of all of the lessons you are exposing yourself to. You need to start taking notes, studying, and reviewing everything you are learning from these lessons. You need to make sure that you are taking lessons from the right people in the first place, and that the lessons you are absorbing are from people who actually know what they are talking about. You also need to make sure that you start practicing these lessons in your own life and that you regularly review how they are working for you so that you can track your progress and increase your success in your own life.

It is easy to complain about the condition in your life when it comes to things like money, your relationship status, your career, your health, or anything else you may be experiencing troubles with. However, it is not easy to actually make changes. It can be difficult to show up to the seminars and conferences that will change your life and actually pay attention, hear what is being said to you, and implement the changes that you are learning about. If you want to see real change in your life, you need to be hungry for that change to the point where you will do everything in your power to satisfy that craving. This means showing up, listening, and turning what you have heard into actual action that you will take to make these changes in your life.

As difficult as it can be to acknowledge it, there is only one person in this world who is capable of holding you back, and that is you. Everything you are experiencing right now is not because you are a victim of your circumstances or a victim of the people around you, it is because you have been unwilling to accept your role as being the leader in your own life. The minute you decide that you are going to lead yourself to greatness and experience change in your life is the minute that you stop playing the victim role in your life and start seeing actual, tangible change. So, what is it going to be? Are you going to read this book, reach the end, and complain that nothing has changed? Or, are you going to read this book, take action, implement change in your life, and finally become the person who leads yourself to greatness? Only you hold the power to answer this question for yourself.

Chapter 2

Learn From Those Who Have Already Achieved Your Goal

If you want to elevate yourself into the next level of your life, you need to start by making sure that you are following people who actually have the capacity to teach you how to do so. One mistake many people make is following mentors who have created a hype around themselves, rather than finding mentors who are actually capable of educating them on how to create change in their lives. The reality is: anyone can build a hype around themselves and get people interested in what they are doing, but only a few people actually possess the ability to teach you what you need to know. If you spend your entire life following the hype, you are likely going to miss out on the highly potent mentors who can teach you what it truly takes to create change in any given area of your life.

How Do You Pick Your Mentor?

Picking the right mentor is crucial as you are going to want to be following people who can actually show you what you need to know and what you need to do in order to create a change in your life. You need to be able to trust that the people you are learning from know what they are talking about so that when you follow what they teach you to do, you can feel confident that you are not wasting your time or energy on these practices. The easiest way to begin identifying the best mentors for you to follow is to look around and identify people who are already doing what you want to be doing. If you want to have a great relationship with your spouse, follow people who have great relationships with their spouses, and look for mentors who experience what you want to experience in your own relationship. If you want to improve your wealth creation and your wealth management skills, follow mentors who know exactly how to create and manage wealth and who are doing so in a way that models exactly what you want to be doing.

Make sure you are picky at this stage and be willing to discern the difference between someone who has something you want, and someone who has something you want *in the way that you want it*. In other words, if you find a mentor who has a great relationship but not a relationship that *you would personally want to have,* they are likely not the best mentor for you to follow. If you find a mentor who has a great ability to create and manage wealth but does not do it in a way that you would personally want to do it, they are likely not the best mentor for you to follow. You need to be as specific as you can when discovering your mentor to ensure that they are going to teach you to have what you *truly* want, and not just a generic version of what you are looking for.

It is important that in addition to finding the right mentor for you, you also find the right number of mentors for you. This is a controversial topic that many will disagree on as there are various ideas around how many people we should follow and learn from at any given time. In my opinion, there are many right answers to this, and the answer that is right for you depends on who you are. The only commonly accepted "rule" in regards to how many mentors you should have is that you should not have too many, and that every single one of your mentors should be clearly and intentionally chosen. Ideally, having anywhere from 1 to 3 mentors is the best number, as this ensures that you will learn plenty and that you will receive everything you need from your mentors. With that being said, you should focus on having just one primary mentor and then having the other 1 to 2 mentors being secondary mentors that help fill in the gaps that the first mentor may leave. If your primary mentor is someone you can regularly meet with in person, these secondary and tertiary mentors may not be necessary because you can easily ask your primary mentor everything you need to know. If, however, your primary mentor is someone you cannot talk to, or that you cannot talk to too much, then having secondary or tertiary mentors is a great way to fill in those gaps so that you truly understand what your primary mentor is teaching.

With all this to be said, understand that every single person is going to teach things differently, even if they are teaching on the same topic. This means that if you have three mentors and you ask all three of them to speak about the exact same thing, all three will have something completely different to say. This is precisely why having a primary mentor is important, as it prevents you from becoming distracted or confused by conflicting knowledge. This way, you are more likely to follow what will actually work, and therefore, you will be more likely to create the results that you desire for yourself.

What Do You Do With Your Mentor?
After you have picked the right mentor for you to follow, you need to become absolutely committed to paying attention to every single thing they do. You need to be willing to pay attention to how they speak, what they say, and how they behave. If you have the pleasure of being able to work directly with your mentor and speak directly to them, do not be afraid to ask as many questions as you possibly can to identify exactly what your mentor does in order to create the results they create. The more questions you ask, the more you stand to learn, and the easier it will be for you to follow what your mentor is teaching you in a meaningful way.

When asking these questions, make sure you do not just ask "what," but you also ask "how" and "why." Knowing how your mentor does something and why they do something is the best way to make sure that you clearly understand the value of this behavior so that you can implement it in your own life. In most cases, knowing the true value and purpose behind behaviors can also help you authentically incorporate it into your own life, meaning you are far more likely to actually create the results you desire. This way, rather than simply mimicking your mentor, you are behaving in a way that they would genuinely behave in during any given circumstance because you know *why* they are choosing the behaviors or the words that they are choosing.

If you do not have direct access to your mentor, you are going to need to do even more work toward understanding and learning from your mentor. You are going to need to take the time to identify why they behave the way they do and how they do it on your own by observing them, paying attention to the results they are creating, and doing your best to develop your own understanding of their words and behaviors. If you can, be sure to also look for answers in any interviews they may be doing or any articles they may write for people who may be asking the very same questions that you are. Learning as much as you can from what they are willing to teach about their methods for success is your best opportunity to absorb as many lessons as you can from your mentor. This way, you will be far more likely to actually implement what they have taught you and begin seeing the tangible results of these changes in your own life.

Chapter 3

Why You Are Where You Are Now and not Where You Would Like To Be

After you find yourself a mentor, it is important that you start at the very beginning of what it takes to truly create a change in your life. The very first step of creating change anywhere in your life is acknowledging that you alone are responsible for where you are right now, and you alone are responsible for the changes that you are going to make in your life. Even if you have an amazing mentor who has all of the answers and who can teach you everything you need to know, if you lack the willingness to personal accountability and responsibility to enforce those lessons, nothing will ever change. Even the greatest teacher in the world cannot inspire change someone who is unwilling to create change from within themselves. Change will only ever come from inside of you. Finding this motivation is key in this process.

If you are truly ready to make a change in your life and you are honestly ready to see something different in your reality, you need to accept and acknowledge this and put it to action before anything else. That way, you are truly available to listen to and learn from every single lesson your mentor teaches you, and you do not waste a single drop of knowledge that they share with you. Remember, if you have chosen your mentor properly, then everything they teach you will be incredibly important, and you will need to be ready to educate yourself on, understand, and act on every single thing you learn about. This starts right from the very beginning of you working with your new mentor.

The Most Important Question: Why Aren't You There Yet?

One of the most important questions you can ask yourself at the beginning of any journey of change is: "Why am I not there yet?" Wording your question this way creates a powerful opportunity for you to take responsibility for the real reason why change has not already happened in your life. Upon acknowledging why change has not happened, you also create the opportunity for you to acknowledge how you can make changes and hold yourself accountable for these changes that you want to be making.

As you answer this question, I deeply encourage you to take to heart the fact that no one and nothing can hold you back without your permission. This means that if you find yourself answering with things like "the economy is not right" or "no one likes me" or anything like that, you need to acknowledge your first problem as being your tendency to pass blame. The reality is: people have made millions in recessions, there is someone out there for everyone, your health can always be improved, and your life can always change. Absolutely nothing fixes us into any given set of circumstances *except* for our own personal unwillingness to believe that change can happen.

Upon answering this question, you will likely discover that the reasons are not as uncontrollable as you might have originally thought, and that change truly can happen. You may begin to realize that these circumstances are things that, with the right effort and time, can be fixed so that they no longer hold you back from having what you want. For example, if one of the biggest reasons is your tendency to pass blame, you can take responsibility for your circumstances, and immediately you take back your power to make change in your life. If one of your reasons is that you do not know how, you can read books, attend seminars, or find mentors who can teach you what you do not know. Virtually everything you may put on your list of why you are where you are right now, and not where you want to be, can be changed as long as you are willing to put the effort in and consistently work toward making those changes.

As you complete this list, make sure that you are as exhaustive as possible. As well, keep the list nearby because it is likely that you will find more reasons as to why you are where you are right now as you go. Often, when you draw your awareness to your own actions that are holding you back, you begin to become more self-aware and find yourself actively acknowledging things that you are doing that hold you back as you do them. Keeping your list nearby ensures that you document these realizations and that you have them in front of you so that you can understand exactly what it is that you are doing on a day to day basis that is keeping you where you are right now. That way, you have a clear list of your "problems" that you need to overcome in order to help you create the life you want to create for yourself. Then, as you begin to overcome these problems, you will find yourself experiencing much greater levels of joy and happiness in your life because you will realize that the problems no longer exist and that you have the power to change any future problems that may arise.

How To Take Responsibility For Where You Are Right Now

After you have created your "master list" of reasons for why you are where you are right now, you need to start taking responsibility for everything you have put on that list. Immediately, you need to acknowledge that you are the one who has made a choice to allow yourself to engage in these behaviors. Even when you realize that some of these behaviors have become nasty habits because you have been doing them so long, you need to realize that it is *you* who has allowed them to become habits, and it is you who has the power to break these habits. There is not one single habit in this world that cannot be broken so long as you are willing to actually put effort into dissolving those habits and creating healthier habits in their place.

The best way to start taking responsibility for where you are right now is to look at the list you have written and read through each of the problematic behaviors and say, "I chose to do that."

For example:

- "I blame everyone else. I chose to do that."
- "I make bad choices with my money. I chose to do that."
- "I struggle to be vulnerable with other people. I chose to do that."
- "I make low-quality food choices, even when I know better. I chose to do that."
- "I use excuses to skip my workouts. I chose to do that."

When you realize that you are the only one making the choices that are leading to you not creating the results you desire, you realize that you are the only one responsible for making changes in your life. In fact, you are the only one who *can* make changes in your life. I can prove that using one simple method: think back to a time in your life where someone was nagging you to do something that you did not want to do. At least one of those times, you willfully chose to ignore that person and refused to do whatever they were asking you to do. No matter what your reasoning was behind it, there was no way that they could change your mind, and you simply did not do it. Maybe you were ignoring your parents asking you to clean your room or your friend who was asking you to go out on a date with someone, or your partner who was asking you to do a chore around the house. No matter who it was and what it was about, you experienced a situation where someone nagged you, and you still willingly refused to do what they told you to do. This is evidence that no matter how hard someone tries, there is no one who can get you into action except yourself. This means that if you want any of those things on your list to change, no amount of someone nagging at you or commanding you to change is going to make a difference in your life. *You* have to be willing to take responsibility and willing to command *yourself* into change, as that is the only thing that will ever make a difference in your life. If you cannot find a way to do that, then you will never find a way to create the changes in your life that you desire and that will help you lead a happier life.

What Do You Do With Your Responsibility?

After you have completed your list of reasons why you are where you are right now and willingly take responsibility for every single thing that has led to you being where you are right now, there is one more activity you need to complete. This activity is going to help you take responsibility for the change you want to create and where you want to end up after you have implemented those changes. It is essentially the same activity; only it comes with an entirely new focus.

To complete this new activity, simply ask yourself: "What could I choose instead?" For example, if your reason behind not changing is that you always pass the blame, ask yourself, "What could I choose instead?" and realize that instead, you could choose to take responsibility. If your reason is that you struggle to motivate yourself to get started, you might instead choose to find ways to motivate yourself. If your reason is that you feel like you are not worthy of change, you might choose to find ways to start feeling worthy. You need to decide what you want to choose instead and make choices that will reasonably offset what you have been choosing so far. This way, you will be far more likely to not only take responsibility for why you are where you are but also take responsibility for the changes you want to make in your life.

After you have completed your list, you are going to do what you did in the previous activity to take responsibility once again by simply saying, "I am choosing to do that."

For example:

- "I used to blame others, but now I am taking responsibility for my actions. I am choosing to do that."
- "I used to make bad choices with my money, but now I am learning how to use my money wisely and manage my money smartly. I am choosing to do that."
- "I used to struggle with being vulnerable, but now I am learning how to let people in. I am choosing to do that."
- "I used to make bad food choices, but now I am learning how to make better food choices and eat a healthier diet. I am choosing to do that."
- "I used to use excuses to skip my workouts, but now I am going to encourage myself and hype myself

up for my workouts. I am choosing to do that."

By consciously making these choices and declaring them to yourself, you begin to change your mindset around how you approach certain aspects of your life. This way, you begin immediately taking responsibility for your choices and for your ability to change the choices you are making to ones that better serve what you desire to create for yourself in life. Then, if you find yourself not making these choices, you recall that the power lies within you and that you can use this power to make a new choice if the choices you are presently making are not serving your goals.

Once you have taken the time to take responsibility for your choices, and for the new choices you are going to be making, you have effectively taken responsibility enough that you can truly absorb what your mentor is going to be teaching you. This way, you become far more likely to learn from your mentor and actually implement these necessary changes in your life so that you can begin to create the life you desire and the results that bring you genuine happiness.

Chapter 4

After Heard, Take Action

If you want to see these changes transpire in your life, you need to know how to make that happen. You know this to be true based on what we have talked about so far, but you may still be wondering what that means and how you can make that happen. At this point, you have effectively taken responsibility and started genuinely listening to your mentor, so now it is time to put all of that knowledge and responsibility into *action*.

This is a step that many struggle with, as taking action is challenging. Knowing how to move forward with what you have been taught, and putting those lessons into action takes a lot more effort than most people realize. This is where you have the opportunity to truly affect change in your life, and it does not come from realizing change needs to happen and understanding what needs to take place in order for change to occur. At this point, you need to be willing to actually take the steps necessary to create changes within your life. If you fail to do so, then realistically, you have still never effectively stepped past the "hearing" stage into "carefully listening." In other words, you have showed up, but you have refused to give the lessons or yourself the energy required to actually create a change within your life. Still, taking those additional steps to actually create change in your life can feel challenging, and I want to address that exact topic right now by showing you how to move from listening to the lessons to actually doing what the lessons taught you.

Why You Are not Immediately Jumping Into Action

Contrary to what you might be thinking, or to what others may have told you, people who fail to take action on the necessary changes in their lives are not failing to do so out of laziness or a lack of desire for change. The belief that laziness or a lack of true desire is what holds people back from making changes in their lives has been a common misconception for years. The truth is, however, that people are actually failing to make changes because they do not know how to work with their natural human processes and their instinctive mindsets to create change. In fact, most people do not know how their mind works at all, which makes it incredibly challenging for them to understand how to work together with their mind to create changes from a base level. If these changes are not created at this deeper level, they will always be temporary, and the person will continually find themselves reverting back to old patterns. Those who do not know better believe that these relapses are indicative of failure or a lack of will to change when, in reality, it is simply a symptom of not knowing better.

The human mind is not as complex as you might think it is. However, it does require certain things to take place in order to facilitate effective and lasting change. Once you understand the human mind, this will become much easier. The number one thing you need to understand about the human mind in order to facilitate change quickly is the development of habits. Habits are necessary for helping your brain complete certain tasks in a systematic way, and with ease. If you did not have habits, your brain would have to exert a massive amount of energy into thinking about what you want to do and doing it all the time. With habits, however, your brain can essentially run on autopilot for all of your habitual behaviors and reserve the rest of its energy for things that require your attention, such as new experiences or experiences that you do not have on a regular basis. By putting everything that you need to do on a regular basis on autopilot, your brain is not required to use as much energy, which is ultimately the goal of your brain overall. This is why habits exist in the first place.

If you do not take the time to understand what habits are and how you develop them, it will be incredibly challenging for you to acknowledge how your brain works and make the necessary adaptations to your methods of change. As a result, you will find that your change is always made on a surface level and requires massive amounts of energy and focus, which, of course, goes against what your brain actually wants to do. Through this, you will find yourself continually falling back into old patterns.

So, if you have been trying to make changes in your life and you find yourself struggling to commit to these changes or continually putting off the changes, chances are this has nothing to do with you being lazy or lacking the desire to actually change. Instead, you are likely experiencing the completely natural process of habit loops, and you have yet to learn about how you can actually change your mind. As soon as you learn how change happens on a deeper mental level, you will be far more likely to be able to facilitate change in your life in a way that is lasting and meaningful.

Understanding the Lifecycle Of Habits and Changing Habits

If habits are at the core of why you are struggling to jump into action with the new changes you want to make, then naturally you are going to need to understand what habits are and how they work so that you can change yours. Fortunately, habits are not challenging to form or break, and the way they work in your mind is actually incredibly easy to understand. Every habit runs on what is called a habit loop, and they are developed by this loop being followed consistently over a period of time, essentially reinforcing each element on the loop.

The four elements of the habit loop include a trigger, a behavior, a reward, and a reinforcement. These four elements of the habit loop need to be repeated a few times over in order for your brain to acknowledge what the trigger means and use it to spark the development of the habit in the first place. As soon as you have reinforced the trigger enough, your brain will begin to naturally run through the process of the habit with you by encouraging you to complete the tasks in the habitual order.

For example, let's say you have the habit of drinking coffee immediately upon waking up. Perhaps you started this years ago as a way to help give yourself some extra energy first thing in the morning so that you could keep up with a busy schedule. Over the years, you have continued the habit, and you may not understand why other than the fact that you "like it." The reality is, at that time in your life, you turned your waking up into the trigger, the act of drinking coffee into the behavior, and the jolt of energy you got became the reward. The thoughts you had following that acknowledged that the coffee helped you wake up would have reinforced the fact that it worked and was a useful habit, and would have reinforced the trigger itself. After repeating this over a few mornings, waking up and having a coffee would become a habit rather than a routine. At this point, if you were to wake up one morning and *not* drink a cup of coffee, it would likely feel weird because you were so used to this habit. For some people, attempting to break the habit this way might even result in them having an "off day" because they started the day off in a way that they were not used to, and which may have made them feel uncomfortable. If they were to look back at what caused them to feel off that day, chances are they would recognize that they had been feeling this way ever since they put off the habit of drinking coffee that morning.

In your life, you have many different habits. Several of these habits you will likely be completely unaware of and will have no idea that they exist or how they support you in living the life that you are currently living. For others, you may recognize them because something has drawn your awareness to them, for example, your realization that they are contributing to you not being able to have what you want in your life. A great example of this would be a habit of blaming others or a habit of procrastinating. If this is happening, you need to acknowledge this habit and take the time to identify the elements of the habit that fall into the habit loop so that you can become aware of the full extent of this habit. This means that you need to become aware of the trigger, the behavior, the reward, and the reinforcement, or reinforcing thoughts.

Once you know the full extent of what your problematic habit is, you can begin to create new habits in its place that will support you with having a better experience overall. The elements of the habit loop you want to focus on changing are the behavior and reinforcing thoughts. The trigger and the reward will generally stay the same since you typically cannot do away with triggers, and the reward is usually as simple as a dopamine release in your brain, which tells your brain what you have done is positive. With this in mind, you will intentionally change the behavior and foster thoughts that reinforce that behavior by thinking about how positive it was and how good it made you feel. As you continue to engage in this change, you will find that your habits naturally begin to change and, as a result, it becomes easier for you to actually take action on things. This is because you are now working within the realm of how your mind works, rather than attempting to override your natural mental processes with willpower, which has been proven time and again to be a useless tactic.

How To Actually Implement What Your Mentor Has Taught You

Now that you understand what habits are and how habits can be changed, you can use this knowledge to help you actually implement what your mentor has taught you. This way, you are no longer holding onto knowledge and never actually using that knowledge to change your life. Instead, you are able to understand how to work with your own mind and behaviors to facilitate the changes you want to see so that you can begin to live the life that you want to live.

You can start implementing what your mentor has taught you by first identifying what habits or behaviors you are engaging in that go against what your mentor has taught you. It is important that you understand what you are doing that is preventing you from already behaving in the way that your mentor teaches you to behave so that you can start removing these problematic behaviors from your life. As soon as you identify these behaviors and any habits associated with them, you can begin to become aware of how they fit into a habit loop. Then, you can become aware of what needs to change in order for you to turn this new behavior into a habit. From there, you simply need to commit to facilitating the change by repeating it on a regular basis and reinforcing your change with as much healthy mental reinforcement as you can.

According to research, it can take at least 21 days to see change in your habitual behaviors and as many as 60 for your new habit to officially take root. This means that you need to consistently work toward intentionally developing your new habit for at least 60 days in order for it to truly become a new habit. If you find yourself wanting to stop or coming up with excuses or reasons for why that habit no longer works for you, chances are you are falling into a pattern of relapse and not an actual experience of realizing that the habit is not helping you. In some cases, the habit may not be helping enough, in which case you can always adapt that habit to get more out of it. However, any adaptations or changes you make should always be highly intentional and should clearly serve you in creating the results you desire to create to ensure that you are doing it with a positive reason. If you cannot clearly explain why these changes are serving the habit of becoming better, or if you feel like you have to work hard to justify these changes, chances are you are making them because you are struggling against your old habits. When this happens, slow down and acknowledge why you are struggling and see if you can do anything to help yourself have a better experience with changing your habits. Perhaps a simple change to your approach to your new behavior or improvements in your reinforcing thoughts is all you need to improve your experience and keep going. As well, you might also consider keeping a "count down calendar" to keep track of the number of days that you have implemented your new habit. This way, you have something to keep you motivated and on track with implementing the changes you need to make in order to create the results you desire to create.

Chapter 5

Define Your Goals

Goals are perhaps one of the most useful things we can have in our lives when it comes to creating changes for ourselves. In a sense, goals are like the oxygen to our dreams in that they are capable of giving us a clear and consistent path forward, which can motivate us and inspire us to stay focused on actually bringing our dreams to life. Having goals is about more than just having dreams: it is about turning those dreams into a step-by-step action plan that allows you to clearly follow that plan and bring your dreams into your reality. If you want to achieve everything you want in life and live a happy life, knowing how to effectively set goals and follow them will be necessary to your success.

In our society, learning about how to actually set goals and pursue them is not something we are generally taught about, but instead, it is something that we have to go out of our way to learn about. This may be another reason as to why so many people fail to ever actually implement the changes they claim they want to implement in their lives. Learning about the purpose of goals, how they work, and how to actually set them will be fundamental in changing your approach to goals forever so that you become far more likely to achieve the goals that you set for yourself. In order to change the way you approach and set goals, however, you must first change the way you define your goals.

Why You Need To Have Goals

Goals are one of the most important things we can have in our lives, as goals reflect our desires, and our desires are implanted within us to give us the motivation to keep moving forward in life. Without desires, we may have no reason to ever change, which means we will always find ourselves living the same old life. I am going to assume that you are not here reading this very book because you want more of the same in your life, but because you actually want to see changes implemented and manifested in a way that is sustainable and lasting. With that in mind, you need to learn how to turn your desires into goals and why.

One of the biggest reasons why you are going to want to set goals for yourself is that it allows you to stay focused. Goals will effectively shut out all of the noise, clarify a path for you to get what you want in life, and allow you to stay completely focused on that path. If you have set your goals properly, you will be able to feel confident that the path you have chosen is the most effective path, and so many distractions or diversions you face along the way will seem irrelevant and unimportant to you. Instead, you realize that the path you have already created is the best path for you and it is the one that is most suited to exactly what you are looking for. As such, you will not be coerced or seduced by the distractions or diversions, and instead, you will be able to stay completely focused on what it is that you are trying to achieve for yourself.

Taking the time to define your goals is also important because your defined goals will provide you with something to hold yourself accountable. Through defined goals, you can recognize anytime you have progressed, identity anytime you have not progressed and identify why not, and otherwise hold yourself accountable for moving forward. A properly designed goal will keep you on track for what you want, so long as you remain committed to seeing it through. Which, of course, if the goal is well-defined and well-designed, it will be.

Goals are easily one of the most motivating and useful tools you can use, and taking the time to define your goals is essential in helping keep you on track for making actual changes in your life. If you are ready to stop dreaming about things being better and start actually making them better for yourself, it is time for you to make some goals.

Using Your Findings To Create Your Goals

Most of us have a pretty good idea of what we want in life, but we often have a slim understanding of what it will take to actually get there. You may be able to identify at least a few of the important steps that it will take for you to get where you want to go, but you may struggle with identifying *all* of the necessary steps. This is where a strong mentor comes in handy as they can help you identify all of the steps you are going to need to take in order to create the results that you want in your life. When you have a mentor, they can fill in the blanks and help give you a clearer understanding of what needs to happen in order for you to get to where you want to be. This way, you are not left wondering or feeling like there are large gaps in your understanding. In many cases, this is the very first step in officially creating your goals because it takes you out of feeling like your goals may be unachievable and puts you in a position where you know exactly what you need to do.

Once you know exactly what you need to do, you need to start actually turning your dreams into goals. This works best once you have these gaps filled in because now you have all of the information that you need to formulate strong and useful goals for yourself so that you can create the results you desire. With all of this knowledge, you know what specifically needs to happen, you know what to measure, you know how to make your goals meaningful, and you know how to motivate yourself to see them through. Naturally, everything you need to generate success exists, and you are ready to make that success come to life.

At this point, I want you to start by taking everything you have learned and simply writing it down on a piece of paper as being your goals. Right now, let's not worry about turning these goals into anything; let's simply focus on you becoming aware of what these goals are and acknowledging how important they are to your success. This is the easiest way to define your goals as it allows you to start by acknowledging what your goals are or what you even want for yourself.

For most people, this is actually where they start and stop. They begin by identifying a vague idea of what they want, or by taking the knowledge they have learned and acknowledging its importance, and then they stop. Of course, nothing happens once they stop because they never actually turned their goals into *goals,* but instead acknowledged them. For this reason, I want you to recognize that we are not going to stop here; this is merely the beginning. With that being said, even something as simple as acknowledging what needs to happen is a great beginning for you as you learn how to then turn this into the process of actually creating useful goals for yourself.

Ensuring Your Goals Align With Your Bigger Picture

After you have acknowledged what your goals need to be, you need to make sure that these goals align with your bigger picture. You can do that by identifying what your biggest goal in life is. Your biggest goal in life is often one of the most complex goals you will have because there will be many things that go into allowing you to have the complete life you want. For that reason, you are going to want to take some time on this activity as you want to make sure that you are thorough and clear on what it is that you are working toward and why.

To start this activity of identifying whether or not your goals fit with your bigger picture goal, let's start by identifying what your bigger picture goal is. You can do this simply by closing your eyes and imagining what your dream life would look like, and then considering all eight areas of your life to ensure that you have a clear understanding of what it is that you want for yourself. While doing this activity, I encourage you to imagine that absolutely zero limitations exist around what you can do and what you can achieve in this life. Imagine that no matter what, you can have virtually anything you want, no strings or conditions attached, and consider what this life would be like.

Start by simply thinking about where you are and what you look like. Then, ask yourself what your wealth would look like, what your career would look like, and what your health would look like. Then, ask yourself what your relationships would look like with your family and friends, what your relationship with yourself would look like, and what your love life would look like. Next, ask yourself what your hobbies would be and how you would nurture your spiritual or religious needs. Once you have asked yourself about all of these eight key areas of your life, open your eyes and write down what you noticed. You should keep this visual of your dream life handy so that you are always able to stay absolutely focused on what it is that you are working toward in the bigger picture.

Then, with this in mind, look at your goals that you have defined for yourself and see if they fit into your bigger picture. Ideally, you should be able to clearly see how every single goal you have set for yourself is going to support you with bringing this bigger picture into your mind. If you cannot clearly see the connection between your goal and your bigger picture, it may be a good idea to set that goal aside and pursue something more aligned in the meantime so that you can get toward what it is that you want to achieve. This will be more time-efficient than spending more time on a different goal that may not be realistic at the moment. The only time you should refrain from setting a goal aside is if your mentor knows what your big-picture vision is and suggests you adopt a certain goal, particularly if they have a life that is similar to your bigger picture. In this case, if the goal does not make sense to you, you should ask your mentor about what the purpose of that goal is so that you can clearly understand why you are pursuing it in the first place.

Chapter 6

The Characteristics Of a Successful Goal

Now that you have defined your goals, I want to take a moment to discuss what makes a goal successful. Goals have a very specific purpose and, as such, need to be developed clearly and intentionally to ensure that they have the power to actually achieve that purpose. If you do not take the time to understand the purpose of a goal and then develop your goals accordingly, then you are going to struggle to ever effectively develop goals that help you move forward in life. What I teach you in this chapter will be useful to help you take those goals you have defined and turn them into something you can reasonably achieve in your life so that you can begin to live the life of your dreams and the life that will bring you the most happiness.

We will be engaging in necessary activities associated with these characteristics in later chapters, so for now, please take the time to read along and understand what goals are meant for and how they need to be developed in order to be successful. You can use your goals as a reference to help you relate to this information and understand it better, but please keep your absolute focus on this book for now. The more intimately you understand the purpose of a goal and the characteristics of a successful goal, the easier it will be for you to complete the necessary practices later on.

What Should a Goal Be In Order To Be Successful?

We have already discussed the value of a goal, which is to have something that clearly defines your path forward and keeps you focused, accountable, and motivated. However, you may be wondering how a goal can achieve so much, especially if you have never taken the time to intimately understand the characteristics of a goal. When a goal is well-developed, all of these benefits and values are *side effects* of that goal as a result of that goal being a successful one.

In order to be successful, a goal needs to be developed in such a way that you feel absolutely confident that it has the capacity to get you where you want to go. This means that you have taken the time to pick a goal that is meaningful to you, and that will help create the results that you want to experience in your life. Then, you have thoroughly researched what steps are required in order for you to achieve those results from that goal. After you have successfully identified what needs to happen in order for those results to be achieved, you need to effectively outline each step that you need to take and turn it into something that is measurable. Then, you need to hold yourself accountable and motivate yourself to stay committed to the task. If the goal is properly developed, it should be easy for you to stay on track, measure your success, and motivate you to keep going because you will be able to clearly see how this goal is bringing you toward what you desire.

In the realm of goal-making, a truly successful goal should be one that is so well-developed that you get everything you need out of it, from the motivation and knowledge to make it happen, to the exact results you were looking for. If all of this takes place, you can celebrate the fact that you have developed a successful goal.

If you are new to goal setting, or if you have never taken goal setting beyond the basic process of identifying your dreams and identifying a few steps that you need to take in order to get there, the idea of creating successful goals may seem overwhelming. It may feel like you are asking a lot from a goal, or like you are trying to create something with no real understanding as to how it is supposed to look in the first place.

Rest assured, the steps I will provide you with are going to support you with getting all the way to the point of creating a highly successful goal that gets you exactly where you want to go.

The steps we are going to cover include creating goals that are specific, measurable, credible, and motivating. Before we get into the activities that will support you in completing these steps, however, we are first going to explore more about what each step is and how it is going to help you cultivate a successful goal in the first place.

A Successful Goal Needs To Be Specific

Having a goal that is specific is perhaps one of the most important and useful characteristics of goal setting that we can take advantage of. Making a goal-specific ensures that you know exactly what you are working toward, which means that you know exactly what needs to happen in order for you to achieve that goal. If your goal is specific enough, you can measure your success, define your milestones, and support yourself in staying motivated. This also ensures that you stay accountable and that you know what to do to keep yourself on track with achieving that particular goal.

When people fail to make a goal-specific, what they end up doing is leaving plenty of room for technicalities, confusion, and a lack of completeness. A goal that is not specific enough can result in you saying things like, "well *technically* I have achieved that goal in doing this," which results in a false sense of security when, in reality, nothing is actually changing. For example, let's say your goal is to eat healthier. If you do not get specific about what you mean, then technically swapping out one sugary beverage for a glass of water each day counts as you eating healthier, even if you are still eating an otherwise unhealthy diet. However, if you got incredibly specific and stated that you wanted to cut out sugars altogether except for three sugary treats *or* beverages per week, then you have something specific to work toward. In this case, you know that if you have already eaten three sugary treats or beverages that week, then you can no longer eat any further sugary treats or beverages that week if you want to remain successful with your goal. Instead, you need to opt for something healthier.

In addition to helping prevent you from leaning into technicalities, having a specific goal to work toward ensures that you know exactly what needs to happen in order for you to succeed because you know exactly what you are working toward. If you did not know exactly what you were working toward, you might find yourself feeling confused or procrastinating ever getting started because you are not absolutely clear on what you are trying to create. Turning your goal into something specific ensures that you know exactly what you are trying to make happen, which means you are less likely to feel intimidated or procrastinate because you know what you need to do. As a result, you are far more likely to see your goal through.

A Successful Goal Needs To Be Measurable

In business, the number one tool that is used for growth in analytics. Analytics are a series of measures that tell a company exactly how they are doing and where they need to focus their efforts on improvements. This also shows them where they are doing great, which, in many cases, allows them to identify what skills they are best at so that they can possibly use those skills to create stronger strategies for the areas where they are presently struggling. When it comes to setting goals, making goals that are measurable allows you to gain a similar benefit from your progress and results. Measurable goals allow you to collect data or analytics about your results so that you can see where you are doing your best, where you need to improve, and what you might do in order to help you improve. The data you will likely collect to support you in measuring your progress and success might include milestones and dates and deadlines. For example, let's say you want to save $12,000 by the end of the year. Your milestones may be set for every $1,000, and you may set those milestones with deadlines at the end of every month. So, on the last day of every month, you should have an extra $1,000 saved up in your bank account. With this measurability, you can track your success, identify where you are doing your best, and discover ways that you may be able to improve upon your ability to save money.

Every single goal that you make should be specific enough that you can clearly identify meaningful and measurable milestones and assign reasonable and effective deadlines to those milestones so that you are motivated to stay on track. Then, you should keep track of what you are doing to achieve those milestones, how quickly you achieve them, and how thoroughly you achieve them so that you can keep track of your progress. Throughout your process of achieving your goals, you can review your progress and compare it against your ideal measurements to see where you are doing well and where you can improve. Then, just like a business, you can use this information to strategize your success and support you in continuing to create the results you desire in your life.

A Successful Goal Needs To Be Credible

Goals that are credible are essentially goals that are meaningful, purposeful, or ultimately desirable to you in your life. They are also goals that are going to be achievable, or that are reasonable in nature. The reality is: if your goal is something you have set because someone else told you to set it, or because you believe it will be a noble goal to have, chances are you are not going to have any connection to that goal. If you do not have any connection to that goal, or you cannot see exactly why it is going to help you get to where you want to go, you will find yourself struggling to create and stay on track with that particular goal. As a result, you might find yourself creating goals that you ultimately never follow through on, largely because you do not care whether you follow through or not. What you may not realize is that while these impersonal and non-credible goals may seem harmless, the reality is that the more you set goals and fail to achieve them, no matter what the reason behind that is, the more this behavior becomes a habit. As a result, you might find yourself struggling to stay on track with your real goals, or the ones that truly matter to you because you have developed the habit of chronically failing to see your goals through. Fortunately, just as with any other habit, you can break it. However, it is easier to never develop this unhealthy habit in the first place so that you never have to face the difficulty of trying to overcome it.

To make your goals credible, make sure that they always align with what you truly want for yourself, and that you can clearly understand why they need to be so important to you. Take the time to really consider how these goals are supporting you, why you care about them, and what you can do to make them matter even more. Even when you are creating goals that you already feel strongly attached to, do everything you can to make them as important as possible. Create your story around why these goals matter and why they need to be non-negotiable for you so that you are more likely to be able to convince yourself to stay on track with these particular goals.

In addition to aligning your goals with what you truly want, you need to align your goals with what you can reasonably achieve. This means that you need to acknowledge what is realistic and what is not, and then measure your goals against those terms. For example, let's say you want to lose weight because you want to feel stronger and healthier in your body. If you were to set the goal of losing 30 lbs in 10 days, this goal would be entirely unrealistic and unachievable, therefore it would not be credible. If, however, you said you wanted to lose 30 lbs in 5 months, that would be far more achievable. As long as you choose goals that are achievable you are far more likely to have the mindset around and connection to those goals that will support you in achieving success.

A Successful Goal Needs To Be Motivating

Lastly, a successful goal needs to be motivating if it is going to be strong enough to keep you on track to seeing that goal all the way through. After all, if a goal fails to motivate you, you are likely going to find yourself struggling to pursue that goal even if you use all of your skills to change your habits and keep yourself committed. Your goals become motivating through two things: the first thing is through a natural effect that happens when you make goals that are specific, measurable, and credible. The process of making goals matter to you and making them clear and easy to follow makes them motivating because it eliminates things like uncertainty, intimidation, and fear around those goals. As well, it ensures that you do not become apathetic toward them, ensuring that you are likely to stay motivated to see them through.

Aside from motivation being something that is naturally built into goals, however, motivation is something you can infuse goals with as well. Ideally, you can to infuse your goals with elements that will motivate you to succeed so that you are more likely to see them through. Only you know what truly motivates you, so only you will know what you can do to make your goals more motivating. This could be anything from embedding certain rewards into certain milestones, making the milestones or the action steps more enjoyable, doing your goal with an accountability partner or a buddy, or doing anything else that motivates you to get into action. No matter what it is, it is important that you juice up your goals with motivating factors so that you are more likely to see them through.

For example, defining as your goal: "I want to earn a million dollars" is a sterile goal, theoretical and therefore not really motivating. Define as your goal: "I want to earn a million dollars (obviously define how, in what time, through which steps) to buy the house of my dreams where to live happily with my family ... to be able to make all the trips I want together with those I love ... to be able to leave a job that it bores me and keeps me busy for too many hours a day and being able to dedicate myself to what I really like to do ... to then be able to make my money work for myself and consequently to be able to spend much more time with my family "... here , I emotionally characterized my goal. This is a moving target! This is a goal that will call me loudly to achieve it!

I HEARD YOU

Chapter 7

A Specific Goal

Now that you know exactly what it takes to make a goal successful, we are going to get into some activities that will help you make your own success goals. As we go through these activities, I encourage you to stay focused on just one single goal that you want to create right now. Once you have successfully created this goal and begun to see it through, you can start applying these very same steps to other goals in your life. It is important to focus on just one thing at a time because you do not want to overwhelm yourself or intimidate yourself by trying to do too much at once. One of the biggest disservices people do for themselves is also a habit they tend to have, and that is to make things so challenging or intimidating that it feels all but impossible to see it through. This often becomes a habit because by making things too challenging or intimidating, they are able to easily create an excuse as to why they have not seen that goal through yet. Of course, the only person that suffers, in the long run, is them because they are only holding themselves back.

With all that in mind, let's start by defining your first goal and then making it specific. This way, you can lay the strongest foundation for this goal possible, which will allow you to turn this goal into something meaningful and successful. As you go through these steps, please make sure that you are completely thorough as the more effective you are during this part of the process, the easier it will be for you to actually see the goal through. Remember, the entire purpose of a goal is to completely plan out everything you need to do so that you no longer have to think about what to do, but instead, you just think about "what's next." The more energy you infuse into this step, the less intimidating or overwhelming the process will seem, which means that you will be far more likely to actually remain committed to that goal and see it all the way through.

Defining the Goal, You Are Achieving

The first thing you want to do is define the single goal that you are achieving. At this point, you have already created a list of goals that is going to support you in creating what you want in your life, so now you need to pick the goal that is going to offer you the most payoff for what you are working toward. By picking the most meaningful goal that is going to get you the biggest amount of growth toward what you want, you ensure that you are automatically picking a goal that is ready to set you up for success. How we think about our goal and how much it excites us, or how much it can offer us if we achieve it, is important to ensuring this element is considered right from the very beginning will help you create the success you want with your goal.

After you have chosen the exact goal that you want to achieve, you need to go ahead and define what this goal is. At this point, you need to clarify what this goal is in a single sentence so that you know exactly what it is that you are working toward. Right now, do not worry about the details or about any of the specifics, just make sure that you can clearly define what this goal is in a single sentence. For example, "I want to read more" or "I want to spend more time in the gym." The goal you are defining right now should support the results you want to create for yourself, which means that you should be able to clearly see how this goal is going to support you in creating the results you desire. For example, reading more will help you learn more and support your mental growth, or spending more time in the gym will help you develop a stronger body.

Once you have defined your goal with a single sentence, I want you to write that goal at the top of a piece of paper. We are going to do a lot more work toward turning this goal into something specific, and then turning it into a measurable, credible, and motivational goal. In order to get there, however, we are going to do this as a step-by-step process that ensures that you are creating strong enough goals that will successfully get you to the results that you truly desire.

Getting Intimate With the Specific Details Of That Goal

With the goal written at the top of your page, I want you to start writing down specific details of what this goal is, what you are trying to achieve, and why you are trying to achieve it. Be as clear as you possibly can, as this is how you are going to be able to develop the specific details of your goal with enough clarity to keep you moving forward.

We are going to start by identifying what the goal is specifically. We are going to start with the specifics of what you are going to be achieving, and follow those specifics all the way down until we have the fine details figured out. So, let's say your goal is to spend more time in the gym because your desired result is to become stronger. At this point, we would follow that goal down to the specific details by first asking, "What will you be doing in the gym?" You could say that you are going to spend time lifting weights, doing push-ups, and otherwise engaging in resistance training to help you develop the ability to become stronger. Now, we are going to go even deeper into detail right now so that later on, when you develop the measurability of your goal, you already have the specifics defined clearly enough that creating the measurability is easy. We are going to do this by asking questions until we come up with the specifics of exactly what you want to achieve. For example, how much stronger do you want to be? How many pounds do you want to be able to lift? How big do you want your muscles to be? Get really clear on what exactly you want to accomplish so that you have the specifics of your goal outlined right from the very beginning.

After you have gotten specific on what you are doing, you need to get specific on what you are trying to achieve. With the aforementioned goal, you are trying to get stronger. You need to be specific on exactly what it is that you are trying to achieve so that you can be clear on why you are pursuing this goal in the first place. Again, make sure that you are as clear as possible when it comes to writing down what you are trying to achieve so that there is no room for guessing or uncertainty. So, if you are trying to save money, clarify what you want to save that money for or what you intend to use that money for in the future. Getting clear on what you are trying to achieve and defining the specifics around what you are trying to achieve right now will ensure that you are laying down strong roots for establishing and developing the credibility of your goal later on.

Next, you want to start to develop the specifics around why you want to achieve this goal. Since specifics are all about laying a strong foundation for your goal, you can recognize this part as being the roots for both your credibility and your motivation behind the goal that you are presently setting. You want to make sure that you are as specific as possible around why this goal is being set so that you clearly understand the importance of this goal for you, which ensures that you know how to approach the development of this goal. When you know why the goal is important to you, creating elements of the goal, such as your milestones, becomes easier because you know what you are trying to achieve. Therefore you know what milestones will be most motivating for you.

Once you have developed these specifics around your goal, you have effectively analyzed your goal well enough and come to understand it well enough that you now know exactly what it is that you are trying to achieve. This information is going to give you an incredibly strong foundation to build out so that you can create a goal that is all but guaranteed to help you create the results that you desire in your life. At this point, you are going above and beyond the basic goal-setting practices that most people use, and you are stepping into practices that are sure to help you win at anything you set out to achieve in your life. This is where you stop being someone who just hears what needs to happen and instead become someone who actually listens to the details and puts those details into work in their own personal lives.

Summarizing Your Specific Goal

The last thing you need to do before moving on with your goal development process summarizes the goal you have created. Now, you have your goal defined, and all of the important details of your goal effectively defined, meaning that you know exactly what it is that you are trying to create. You want to take all of this information and turn it into one single sentence that is clear, concise, and that leaves absolutely no room for confusion or loopholes so that you know exactly what it is that you are trying to accomplish. The more focused you can make this summarizing sentence, the easier it will be to build out your goal and keep yourself on track. Even if there is a lot of information behind what your goal is, why it is important to you, and what your desired results are, it is crucial that you keep this sentence as easy and to-the-point as possible. The rest is still important, but including it all right now can make your goal feel overwhelming and intimidating and can actually hold you back from achieving it.

The best way to summarize your goal is to simply follow this formula by filling in your own information as per your own goal:

- "I want to (achieve these results) by (doing this) (because of this.)"

For example:

- "I want to become stronger by lifting weights in the gym because I like how strong muscles make me look."
- "I want to eat healthier by learning to cook better meals because I desire to have more energy and better overall health."
- "I want to save $12,000 by the end of the year by putting away $1,000 per month because I want to have security funds in case anything should go wrong."

Tailor these specifics to your own goal so that it clearly represents what you are working on. Again, make sure you are specific as possible and keep it as clear as you can in one sentence or two at most. Keep the long-winded explanations and justifications out of this part because they are not relevant to the goal making process.

Chapter 8

A Measurable Goal

With your goal's foundation locked in place through the specifics, the next thing you need to do is build out the measurability of your goal. At this point, you want to start turning your goal into something that you can clearly turn into a step-by-step action plan and that you can easily measure to ensure that you are making decent progress toward your goals. If you did the specifics step right, building out your measurements should be effortless because you should already have a clear understanding of exactly what it is that you are trying to achieve. At this point, you simply need to assign measurements to it, break those measurements down into steps, and assign deadlines to each step you develop. This way, you have clear "data" that you can use to help measure your progress and to support yourself with staying on track or, if necessary, creating new strategies so that you can get back on track.

When it comes to creating the measurements of your goals and breaking them down with deadlines, there is one element you need to be very intentional about including so as to avoid turning your goal into something that is overwhelming or intimidating. It is natural for your overall goal to seem big or intimidating, but applying measurements and breaking it down should be the part of the process that helps you realize that your goal is actually achievable. This is the point where you get to visually and reasonably see that your goal can be achieved so long as you are willing to work on it just one step at a time. That element you need to consider is reality. You need to make sure that the measurements you set and the deadlines you create are reasonable and that you are not trying to push yourself to achieve more than is realistically possible at any given time. Attempting to create goals that are unrealistic, or at least unrealistic to you, will result in you seeing your goal as being unachievable. When you see your goal as unachievable, you immediately check out and stop putting any effort into making any progress because your default state of mind becomes "what's the point?"

Keeping your goal's measurements and expectations realistic ensures that you begin to see how successful you can really be with this goal. With that in mind: create measurements and deadlines that challenge you but excite you. If, at any point, your measurements or deadlines begin to seem unreasonable or unachievable, you need to acknowledge this and adjust your measurements and deadlines to assure that they can actually be accomplished. Otherwise, they will never serve you in getting where you want to go. A great way to make sure that you are keeping your goals realistic is to start by getting measurements and deadlines and then stepping away from your goal for a little bit before coming back and reviewing the measurements and deadlines you have set. At this point, you should ask yourself if they seem reasonable and achievable, or if you need to make them a little more challenging or a little less intimidating. Adjust them as needed to ensure that you have measurements that match what you are trying to accomplish.

For example: "I want to get rich" is not a measurable goal; it is a desire, a dream, not a goal. "I want to earn a million dollars in 4 years by dedicating myself to the real estate sector, trading and a network" is a measurable and realistic goal!

"I want to be thin" is a desire, not a goal. "I want to lose 10 pounds in a year" is a measurable, therefore achievable goal!

Using Your Specifics To Define Your Measurements

To define the measurement of your goal, you need to look at your specifics. Think about what you are trying to achieve, why you are trying to achieve it, and what results you would like to experience from your goal. Then, assign a form of measurement to your goal. Make sure this measurement is clear and easy to actually measure so that you know exactly what you are working toward when you begin working toward your goal. Some great measurements include weight, size, dollars, quantity, and time. Make sure that you clearly specify your measurement so that you know exactly what your ideal final measurement should be.

Examples of specific measurements could include:

- "Lose 10 pounds."
- "Gain 1 inch."
- "Save $5,000."
- "Earn 10 new customers."
- "Sleep 8 hours."

After you have created your ideal measurements, you need to assign a deadline to your measurements. Your deadline ensures that you know when you want to have that measurement achieved by so that you feel a sense of urgency to get started. If you do not take the time to assign a deadline to your goal, you will never get started because you will never feel any pressing reason to actually start. In setting your deadline, do not be afraid to make it one that makes you feel somewhat nervous as this nervousness will give you the energy you need to get started. Your goals should be somewhat intimidating so that you feel challenged to get started, but it should still be realistic. For example, if you make $4,000 a month, saving $5,000 in 12 months might seem intimidating, but it is certainly possible. However, if you make $4,000 a month, saving $5,000 in 2 months is unlikely to be achievable, considering you still need to cover your living expenses. The key here is to make sure your goal still feels realistic even if it does pressure you into trying harder and staying incredibly focused in order to achieve it. If your measurement and deadline encourages a sense of competition or challenge within you, it has done exactly what you need it to do. If not, you may need to adjust your measurement and deadline to ensure that they fit your needs and support you with developing a successful goal.

Identifying Your Goal's Milestones

After you have defined the final measurement and deadline for your goal, you need to break your goal down into milestones. This is where you are going to identify the stepping stones that you need to take in order to get you to your goal. Your milestones will serve as a series of mini-goals that support you in getting all the way to your bigger goal, so you need to take them just as seriously as you do your end result. Since the purpose of a goal is to completely plan everything out at first so that you do not need to touch the plan again later on but instead simply see it through, you want to be very thorough at this part. The more realistic and effective you can plan out your path, the more likely you will be to follow it all the way to your results.

You can see the milestones of your goal as being no different than the landmarks on a paper map when you are trying to find your way to a specific destination. If you know what landmarks you are looking for, you can easily make your way to each landmark and then pivot toward the next landmark. If, however, you are unclear as to what these landmarks are, they are not well defined, or they are not realistic, chances are you will miss them, and as a result, you will never end up at your destination. The same goes for milestones. If you make milestones that are clear and realistic, you will be able to achieve them and then immediately pivot all of your focus and energy into your next milestone. If, however, your milestones are unclear or unrealistic, you will struggle to effectively follow them to get to your final destination.

With that being said, take a look at your destination and think about reasonable milestones you can cultivate out of your destination. Typically, this should be smaller chunks of your goal that are evenly distributed and that inspire you to feel challenged to step into action, but do not feel unachievable. They should feel even easier than your actual goal since they are just bite-sized pieces and not quite as large or as intimidating as your overall goal. Upon defining your milestones, you should first define the measurements you will use to create these milestones, and then define the milestones themselves.

For example, if you want to lose 9 pounds in 3 months, your milestones might be to lose 3 pounds per month, which reflects your measurements used to create your milestones along the way. With that measurement in mind, you can clearly define your first milestone as being 3 pounds lost in the first month, your second milestone as being 6 pounds lost in the second month, and your third and final milestone as being 9 pounds lost in the third month. This creates a clear and simple path for you to follow and also clearly outlines exactly what results you should see, by when.

It is important that you do the math early on to identify what each milestone should specifically be, especially if you are working on larger goals such as ones that will take several months or even a year or more. This way, you always know exactly what final result you should have at any given time, which ensures that you are making adequate progress toward your goals. As well, you should keep track of your milestones, particularly when it came to when they were achieved so that you know how effectively you are reaching these milestones and whether or not they have been properly distributed.

If you find yourself achieving milestones too quickly, chances are you have not created big enough milestones, or you have given yourself too much time to achieve these milestones. Reducing the size of the milestone or tightening up on your deadlines is a great opportunity to make sure that they serve you and keep you moving in the right direction. If you find that you are consistently not achieving your milestones, however, you may need to either adjust your milestones *or* adjust your strategy for achieving your milestones. In some cases, you may find that your milestones are completely reasonable, but you have been using a poor strategy in helping you actually achieve those milestones. In this case, you want to fix your strategy so that you are more likely to be able to achieve them. Alternatively, if you find yourself feeling as though you have been using the best possible strategy and you are making progress, you are simply not making it as quickly as you had hoped you would, you can adjust your deadlines accordingly. At this point, you will want to be more lax on your deadlines, but you should still keep them tight enough that they motivate you to stay in action. You do not want to relax your deadlines so much that they start to feel far away, as this can promote procrastination and further reduce your success rates.

Adapting Your Milestones To Your Personal Needs

Once you have clearly defined your measurements and deadlines and drawn up all of your milestones, the last thing you need to do is adapt your milestones to your own personal needs. Adapting your milestones to your personal needs ensures that your goals are able to fulfill what you are truly looking for and that you are more likely to actually achieve these milestones. Only you will know what is going to motivate you to achieve your milestones, so you need to take the time to identify what matters to you, what motivates you, and what feels realistic for you. As well, if you have any external influences inspiring you to achieve this goal, you can factor them in. For example, if you are getting married and you want to be a certain weight so that you fit into your dress or tuxedo by your wedding day, you might set milestones for what your measurements will be like on your fitting day for getting your clothes fitted. Or, if you are planning on saving money, you might set certain deadlines and milestones that help you incorporate a family vacation or a special trip into your savings plan.

Considering these special milestone requirements and influencers ensures that the milestones you create for yourself are personalized to your needs, motivate you, and inspire you to understand why they are so important. They also develop a sense of urgency, which helps you stay focused so that you are more likely to consistently complete the various steps of your goals.

After you have effectively incorporated your personal needs and preferences into each milestone, you can consider your measurements for your goal complete. At this point, you know exactly what it is that you are trying to achieve, and you know what milestones you are going to need to achieve in order to get there. Now, all you will need to do is pursue those milestones consistently so that you achieve them and stay on track for your goals.

Chapter 9

A Credible Goal

At this point, many people will consider their goals made and ready to be pursued, but truly successful people know that there are two additional steps needed to create successful goals. The first very important step is that in order to have very high chances of being achieved, a goal must be credible, that is, realistic, objectively achievable (albeit with commitment and hard work). The second fundamental step is to precisely define one or more reasons why your goal is really important to you, the motivation to achieve this goal. This is where you begin to reasonably justify your goal and explain why it is so important to you so that you can really give yourself everything you need to achieve your goal.

The reason why you need to place so much energy into developing a credible and motivational goal is that you already know you are going to run into difficulties, and these difficulties are going to possibly hold you back from achieving your goals. If you can acknowledge these difficulties in advance and offset them by having massive meaning behind your goals, you can encourage yourself to stay on track even when it feels hard. Developing your meaning early on gives you a strong reason as to "why" you are doing what you are doing and keeps you focused. This is a secret that is used by the most successful business people, athletes, and overachievers in the world, and it is a secret that can help you officially create those changes you have been longing for, too.

Creating Goals That Are Realistic
When it comes to creating goals in your life, you need to assess your goals and consider whether or not they are truly realistic. One way that many people sabotage themselves

in their ability to successfully achieve their goals is by setting goals that are entirely unrealistic. If you set a goal that is unrealistic, you immediately know this to be true and right from the start you will be less likely to put effort in and to work toward actually achieving what it is that you desire. As a result, you will find yourself creating a poor mindset around your goals right from the start because your goals will intimidate you or will seem obviously impossible.

Rather than setting yourself up for failure, set yourself up with something that is realistic. One of my favorite sayings is: "set your goals high and your milestones low." This essentially means that you can certainly have lofty goals, but you need to be realistic in your ability to achieve those lofty goals. If you want to earn 1 million dollars, for example, it is extremely unlikely that you will be able to do so by the end of the month. If, however, you were to aim to make 1 million dollars in 5 years, that would be far more realistic and achievable. Give yourself plenty of room and realistic milestones to help you achieve the goals you desire to achieve and, with enough time, you will be able to achieve anything.

If you are setting a goal and you are not entirely sure as to whether it is credible or realistic enough, stop and look at it honestly. Assess the facts and ask yourself if it truly is possible for you to achieve that goal. If you have to tell yourself "of course, anything is possible" chances are you have set a goal that is a little too high and you need to be more realistic, or give yourself a longer deadline. If, however, you can say "of course, that is plenty of time to accomplish that particular goal" then you have likely set a goal that is large enough and with a healthy enough deadline.

Getting Clear On Why You Care

Getting clear on why you care is about more than just saying why you want to do something. At this point, you need to develop a real reason behind why you care so that you can encourage yourself to genuinely feel for the significance and purpose of your goal. You want to feel like you know *exactly* why your goal matters so much to you so that when you feel like saying no or giving up on parts of your necessary action steps, you can consider these important reasons behind why you care so much. When you are able to recall these important reasons, you are more likely to actually motivate yourself to stay on track because you can see exactly why your goal needs to come to life in the first place.

This is the part where you want to justify your goal to yourself as much as you possibly can, and you want your justifications to actually matter. You should feel some sort of emotional attachment to your justification to ensure that you genuinely *feel* the importance and significance of the goal you have set for yourself. The more you can create this feeling within you, the more likely you will be to keep yourself motivated to stay on track with your goals.

The truth is, you should never create a goal that you cannot define as credible and meaningful to your bigger picture, and to you as a person. If you find yourself attempting to justify goals that are noble but that have no clear significance to you or value to your life, you will likely find yourself still struggling to see those goals as being important. With that being said, you need to make the meaning of your goals as personal as possible. If you are doing them for someone important in your life, that is entirely fine. Make sure you define *why* that person is important and why these goals are important, too, so that you always remember why they need to be accomplished.

As you create the credibility and meaning around your goal, aim to create at least three reasons behind why you want to achieve your goal. Having a few strong reasons to fall back on ensures that you always remember that your goal has a massive value behind it that will significantly improve your ability to stay focused and keep moving forward. Think of these additional meaningful reasons as being your "insurance" so that you can never justify why you *can't* pursue your goal. If you do happen to find a loophole or a way to justify your way out of one of those reasons, the additional two or more will stand to show you that there is no reason valid enough to stop you from moving forward.

Aligning Your Goal and Action Steps With Your Bigger Picture

Lastly, you need to align your goal with your bigger picture. Ideally, your bigger picture goal should have the most emotion, meaning, and purpose behind it. This should be the goal that moves you to excitement, fear, and hope all at once by showing you what is possible for you and putting everything you truly and deeply want in front of you. If you have defined your bigger picture well enough, you should be able to rely on it to always motivate you to stay in action because of how much it truly means to you.

Knowing how important your bigger picture goal is to you, you should be able to use that to ensure that your smaller goals will have massive meaning for you, too. In fact, simply acknowledging that these smaller goals will move you toward that bigger life goal should be plenty to inspire you to stay in action. However, because you know that it can be easy to talk yourself out of things, you are going to make sure you have plenty of valid, meaningful reasons behind why you need to accomplish this particular goal.

By the time you are done defining the reasons behind why your goal is so important and establishing it as being credible and worthy, you should have a strong case serving your goal and inspiring you to get it done. These reasons should feel so personal to you that they feel as though they grab on your heart and pull you in the very direction of your milestones and success. If your reasons do not compel you to feel emotionally charged by and involved with your goal, they are not strong enough, and you need to go back and discover new reasons to keep you motivated. You should absolutely never question the meaning behind your goal after completing this step, as this step should be the one that takes your goal from being a good idea to a non-negotiable goal.

Chapter 10

A Motivating Goal

The final element your goal needs to have is the power of motivation. As I previously mentioned, if you completed the last three steps of your goal development process properly, your goal should already be fairly motivating. After all, it should clearly define what you are working toward, feel achievable, and have a strong emotional reason behind why it matters to you. All of these things should come together to help you see why your goal is so important and why you should see yourself as being capable of achieving that goal.

With that being said, I want to remind you about something we talked about much earlier, which is the human condition and our tendency to prefer habits over anything else. Until now, all of your habits have inspired you to behave the way you already behave, which is why you have not already achieved your goal. If you want to change that reality, you need to discover what motivates you and further infuse your goal with motivational elements to ensure that you stay absolutely committed to seeing your goal through. Consider this as being even more insurance toward you, creating a goal that is a non-negotiable and a no-brainer. When you effectively develop motivational elements of your goal, you truly keep yourself inspired to keep going because you make it so easy to do so, and it becomes such a massive reward to keep pursuing your goal.

Developing the motivational parts of your goal is going to start by identifying what already motivates you in your goal and accentuating it. Then, you are also going to identify what motivates you personally and use that to increase the number of rewards you gain out of your goal, which will further motivate you to stay on track. All of this can be done by looking at what you have already created for yourself, and by considering your personal needs and preferences and putting that all together into a goal that you cannot help but succeed at achieving.

Identifying the Motivational Parts Of Your Goal

Upon choosing to turn your goal into something that is incredibly motivating, you need to first identify what areas of your goal already motivate you. This could be anything from how important this goal is to you, to how achievable this goal is and how easy the milestones seem based on how you have made them. These are all-natural built-in elements of motivation that you have successfully designed along the way, allowing you to keep yourself inspired to stay on track and see the goal all the way through.

At this point, I want you to see if you can enhance these motivational elements of your goal even further. We are going to consider additional steps you can take to turn these rewarding elements into something even more rewarding, meaning that you are actually raising the stakes and therefore increasing your incentive to succeed. Your primary goal with this step is to make the rewards even better, which will naturally make the process of failing at your goal seem even worse because you will risk losing even more. As you do this, however, you realize that the milestones are still reasonable, and the goal is still achievable, so while the loss would be worse, it is also still reasonable to believe that you will not actually lose. This way, you stay even more motivated to stay on track.

Some things you could do to improve your rewards include developing affirmations for yourself that help you feel even better, offering yourself simple rewards such as special dates or treats you might offer yourself, or otherwise infusing these rewards with something that excites you.

Make sure these rewards genuinely activate excitement within you so that you are more likely to stay motivated to achieve them. You really want to activate the reward center within your brain so that you turn the process of achieving your goals into a habit as well, which will further support you in achieving future goals.

Infusing Your Goal With Motivational Qualities

In addition to accentuating the existing motivational portions of your goal, you also want to add more things that make your goal motivating for you. This means that you are going to identify new ways that you can inspire yourself to stay on track by acknowledging yourself and celebrating yourself along the way. Often, this includes creating a secondary set of milestones that you will follow complete with their own unique rewards, which will further motivate you to stay on track.

For example, if you are trying to save $1,000 per month, you may already have a reward system in place for each month that you save $1,000. However, you may want to include an additional reward system that says every week that you successfully put some money aside into a savings account, you will reward yourself with something. This could be a coffee date, a special bath with your favorite bath products, a small present you buy yourself such as a new book or something similar, or anything smaller that motivates you to keep going. Ideally, these smaller rewards should happen regardless of how much progress you have actually made, and so long as you have worked toward your goal consistently every single day.

Creating these smaller rewards incentivizes you to stay on track even if you do not find yourself creating the results you desire. The more you can reward yourself for staying on track and motivate yourself to keep going, the more likely you will be to put all of your effort into achieving this goal. This means that even if you do not see your desired results early on, you will start seeing them later on because you will be motivated to find a new strategy, develop a better plan for your goal, or otherwise see your challenges through. The more motivated you can keep yourself, the more you guarantee that you are going to see results no matter what.

If you are not entirely clear as to what feels like a reward for you and what is going to motivate you to stay on track, this is a great time to start getting to know yourself better. You can use your next goals as an opportunity to test out different rewards to see which ones you like most; then, as you start to understand what feels like a genuine reward for you, you can begin to intentionally incorporate those rewards into future plans. This way, all of your future plans will start out being even more exciting from the beginning because you knew exactly how to develop them in such a way that kept you motivated.

In fact, that is one of the biggest lessons you can learn about goal making is that the art of goal making truly is a skill within itself. While goals themselves are tools, developing goals properly and in a way that keeps you moving takes time and practice. You need to be willing to keep trying and to keep learning about yourself and the process so that each future goal you make is even more successful, and you develop even better results every single time. Chances are, the very mentors you are following right now have been setting and achieving goals for a long time, and that is why they make it look so easy. You, too, can have this much ease in your own goal setting if you are willing to keep trying and seeing your goals through no matter what.

Chapter 11

The Importance Of Chunking Down

Believe it or not, you have already been effectively chunking down your goals if you have followed every step to this point so far. You have effectively taken your bigger picture goal and turned that into a series of several smaller goals, then you took those smaller goals and defined them and gave them milestones. Chunking down goals is a necessary step that you need to take if you are going to be able to effectively achieve these goals because it takes something that may otherwise seem intimidating and turns it into something achievable. The idea is that each smaller chunk seems so easy that you have no problem achieving it, and that creates sensations of instant gratification. That instant gratification builds momentum and keeps you working toward the larger things like your milestones, your goals, and your bigger picture.

Although you have already done so much work in breaking your goal down into milestones, there is more you can do to further break your goal down and make it even easier. That is, you can take those milestones and break them down into action steps that you can follow so that you know exactly what you need to be doing from moment to moment. Earlier I talked about the metaphor of your milestones being like a map to your destination, and if we were to elaborate on that, then using "chunking it down" as a method to creating action steps would be akin to learning how to move yourself toward the landmarks. If you were driving a car, this would be the same as learning about where the gas pedal and brake pedals were and how to steer the vehicle. If you were walking, this would be the same as learning to move your feet and follow the map all the way to each landmark.

Breaking down your goal into steps is easy, and it will help you turn your milestones into action steps that you can put on your daily to-do lists. If you want to be successful at achieving your goals, I highly recommend including this step in your goal development and achievement process.

Eating the Elephant One Bite at a Time

There is an old Chinese proverb that states, "A man can eat an elephant if need be, one bite at a time." In pop culture, this has been turned into a question: "How do you eat an elephant? One bite at a time." This saying goes a long way in helping you see the value of chunking down your goals so that you can effectively get through them. Goals themselves, and even milestones, can seem intimidating and lengthy. Many of us have developed unhealthy relationships with setting and achieving goals, and as a result, we find ourselves regularly skimping out on achieving our goals. You might find that even with incredibly easy goals and milestones, you find yourself looking for reasons why you cannot follow through, or you simply fall back on procrastinating until it seems like there is no way you can achieve that goal in a reasonable amount of time. This is not an uncommon experience for people to achieve, and it is often rooted in feeling like the goal is overwhelming, even if you have already done the work of breaking it down into bite-sized pieces.

Chunking it down allows you to further take that goal and turn it into even smaller and even easier pieces for you to complete. The idea here is that you want to make the steps seem so easy that there is no reason why you can't achieve them. Then, you want to place those steps on your to-do list. From there, you want to use the meaning behind the metaphor of eating an elephant one bite at a time by truly focusing on just one step at a time. While you can use the bigger picture and your meaning and motivation to keep you moving, at this point, you should focus only on what you have to do next. Then, once you achieve that next step, focus on what you have to achieve after that.

The process of keeping your mind hyper-focused on just one step at a time is one that takes skill and practice, and one that will go a long way in helping you achieve your goals. In doing so, you prevent yourself from becoming overwhelmed or intimidated and procrastinating because you stop focusing on everything and start focusing on the one easy little thing that you can do. Then, when you are done that, you focus on the next easy little thing that you can do. You simply repeat this process over and over until you are done.

In order to really make this work for you, you really need to practice just focusing on one step at a time. Even if the bigger picture excites you and makes you feel ready to jump into action, be ready to put that image and excitement aside and focus exclusively on one little thing at a time when it comes time for you to actually step into action. The better you get at training your mind to stay focused like this, the less likely you are to let that excitement turn into overwhelm and hold you back.

Chunking Your Goal Down Into Action Steps For Your To-Do List

Ideally, you should cultivate a systematic process for how you are going to chunk down the milestones of your goal so that you can turn it into action steps and put it on a to-do list. This process ensures that you are not spending too much time focusing on the bigger milestones and that, instead, you are focusing on exactly what needs to get done. The best practice for making this happen is looking at your next milestone and turning that milestone into a series of action steps and then scheduling those action steps out into your day to day schedule. Then, once you are done, put the milestone away and stop looking at the bigger picture and simply follow those steps. If you find yourself feeling unmotivated to complete a step or feeling like you are trying to justify your way out of doing the work at any given time, use your credibility and motivational practices to get yourself into action. Otherwise, simply stay focused on getting everything done on your to-do list.

Once you finish that milestone, you can go back to looking at the next milestone, turn it into a series of action steps, and then put those action steps into your calendar. Again, put the bigger picture away after that and go back to being exclusively focused on what needs to get done. This may seem unnecessary, but trust me when I say it will prevent you from becoming intimidated or overwhelmed so that you can stay completely focused on getting your job done and making progress.

Even most businesses do not do incredibly thorough daily analytic checks but instead have intentional "checkpoints" where they check-in to see how well they are doing and then adjust their process after that. The reason behind this is that you could have an off day, you could need time for the momentum to build, or you could simply need more time for things to click into place. Either way, over-analyzing yourself and your results can massively hold you back and make you feel like you are not doing good enough even when you are doing great. Rather than analyzing yourself into a state of analysis paralysis, commit to keeping your analysis practices more intentional and thought out so that you are not overwhelming or intimidating yourself into inaction.

Chapter 12

The Importance
Of Acquiring a Method

Have you ever heard the phrase "don't try to reinvent the wheel?" If so, then you may know exactly what I am going to say within this chapter. Even so, it is important that I bring this information to your awareness to remind you that there is no reason why you should have to attempt to reinvent the wheel by doing things your way. After all, your way is what you have been doing so far, and as a result, it has gotten you to where you are now, right?

Learning how to lovingly accept that your own way is not the best way is an important step in letting yourself move beyond the results you have already created for yourself so that you can achieve something even greater in your life. After all, what you have already done may have gotten you to where you are now, but trying something new is the key to get where you are going next.

Acquiring a method when it comes to how you approach your goals and growth in life is not just about letting go of what you have already been doing so far so that you can create something different in your life. It is about mindfully and intentionally identifying what you can do instead to create the different results that you desire. You need to feel absolutely confident that the new method you are choosing is going to have the capacity to take you where you are going. Otherwise, you may find yourself wasting your time. Using the wrong method is more likely to get you more of what you do not want rather than more of what you do want. The reality of it is: the tried and true methods *work,* so use them to your advantage and leverage them to get you where you want to go.

Turning Back To Your Mentor

The first step in acquiring a new method for achieving your goals is to turn back to your mentor. At this point, you should already feel confident that the mentor you have chosen has the capacity to get you where you want to go, so it should be easy enough for you to begin following what they teach you. However, you may find that after outlining and defining your goals, you realize that there is more that you want out of life beyond what your current mentors may be able to teach you. If this is the case, make sure you spend time finding a new mentor who can help you get exactly what you want more of in your life so that you can get more. If you find yourself in search of a new mentor, make sure you find one that accurately reflects what you want and what you want to know more about so that you can gain access to the information you truly need to succeed.

After ensuring that your mentor can still give you the information that you need to succeed, you need to go ahead and start working with your mentor. This is when you are going to start really taking the time to truly listen to what your mentor is saying and observe what your mentor is doing so that you can understand exactly what it is that they are doing that results in the success they are experiencing.

You want to make sure that you are highly intentional in listening to them without attempting to change any of what they are saying as a result of your own bias. This is a massive mistake that many mentees make is that they listen to what their mentor is saying, but then they try to become inventive and create their own ways to implement what their mentor is teaching them. When you are learning something new is no time to be improvising to try to recreate what your mentor has created "in your own way." If there are elements of this method that you can customize, trust that your mentor will tell you exactly what those methods are and how you can customize them to suit your own needs. Eventually, in time, you will be able to adapt the methods for your own use, but as you are just learning them, you do not yet have the intimate knowledge that you need to understand the value of each step and how it may be modified without changing your results.

When you first start practicing these changes in your life, make sure you are copying exactly what your mentor tells you to do, even if it seems entirely irrelevant to what you are trying to accomplish. If they tell you to change your morning routine, for example, and your goal is to change your financial status, then trust that changing your morning routine is something you must do. It is not uncommon for unusual things to directly impact certain results in our lives, and, being that your mentor has already produced those results, it is likely that they know exactly what those uncommon things are. If you desire to produce the results that your mentor has effectively produced, then you need to follow even the uncommon or unlikely things to see those results in your own life, too.

If you ever find yourself confused about why something needs to be done or the value of a certain practice, do not be afraid to ask or spend more time observing how that particular practice contributes to your mentor's results. A good mentor will always take the time to either tell you or show you why that practice is crucial because they know that understanding why something is important is just as valuable as understanding what it is and how to do it. The more you ask questions, the more informed you will be, and the more effective you will be at implementing what you have learned.

You should absolutely never try to modify your method of approach after your mentor has taught you until you have started consistently producing results of your own. At that point, you may start to recognize areas in your own success where you can improve your approach and receive even better results. However, until you begin to consistently create the results you specifically want, you will lack the necessary knowledge to know how to properly adapt or modify your approach without sabotaging your results. Much of the intimate understanding of these methods comes from actually having applied them and received results, not just from hearing about what they are and attempting to modify them early on. Until you have created the results yourself on a consistent basis, you simply do not know enough about the method itself to be qualified to make any changes in the way you apply that method. Do not do it! Stay the course and watch as your results begin rolling inconsistently over time.

Implementing the Methods Your Mentors Use

The best way to begin implementing the methods your mentors use is to do so immediately upon hearing about those methods. Learning through actual action is often the best way to create change in your life because it allows you to physically experience what that change is and visually see what those changes lead to.

As you begin implementing the methods your mentor's use, make sure that you pay close attention to everything they are doing to make those methods work. You want to do your best to mimic every single part of the method, even the subtle parts that seem completely pointless to you. Everything from what you do to how you do it matters, and you want to do your best to ensure that all of these subtle nuances are being done properly to help you get the exact results you are looking for.

The best method for actively learning from your mentor is as follows: ask a question, hear the answer, write it down, implement the answer, perfect the change, write it down, and start over again. You will do this again and again as you continue to implement each of the changes your mentor teaches you about so that you can create the results you desire to create in your life. If you find yourself struggling with anything, such as understanding and implementing the changes, always go to your mentor and ask them for support in how you can approach that particular change. They themselves may have also experienced difficulties in that area of their method, and so they may have additional support they can offer you to help you make the changes you want to make in your life.

So, you will start by telling your mentor what it is that you want to accomplish in your life and then ask them what the next best thing is for you to work on so that you can start making those changes in your life. Then, you will write down the answer they give you. You want to make sure that you are clearly listening and that the notes you take accurately reflect exactly what they said, and not just what you wanted to hear so that you know specifically what you need to be doing. Then, you need to go implement that action into your everyday life as per their recommendation and start perfecting it. This is where you can ask questions and begin to observe your own behaviors to see how you can implement that action even better. If you find yourself struggling to implement it, start by looking within yourself and seeing why that is the case. Maybe you can work on some personal skills around things like better communication, holding yourself accountable, or healing personal issues you may be dealing with that are holding you back. If you do this and you still find you are struggling, then request some support for your mentor in helping you overcome these struggles. Make sure you take notes through all of this so that you can understand exactly what is going on, and you can keep track of any experiences you might have along the way. This way, if you run into troubles, later on, you can follow these notes to identify exactly what challenges you might be facing overall and how you can overcome those challenges to help you find your way through. After you have implemented your change and started to see some results, you can go back to your mentor and begin to receive direction for even more change. This way, you will be ready for the next step and you can continue building on the method that you have already been given. As you continue to follow these steps exactly as your mentor describes them and directs you to you will find yourself experiencing exceptional results from your new method, allowing you to get even closer to what you actually want in life.

Chapter 13

Kill Your Fears

As you go through the process of implementing your new method and pursuing your goals in life, it is absolutely guaranteed that you are going to experience fears. Not one person in this world is exempt from experiencing fears, not even the people you would consider to be the most brave or courageous people that you know. Taking the time to understand this and accept this will allow you to acknowledge that facing your fears is an inevitable part of growing and creating the results you desire. If you want to get to your dream life and all of the happiness you could ever ask for, you need to find a way to acknowledge and face your fears along the way.

What Are Fears, Really?

Fears are essentially experiences we have that prevent us from taking action on certain things in our lives. On a biological level, fear helps us recognize when something may or may not be dangerous so that we can avoid putting ourselves at risk of being endangered. As a species, however, we have advanced to the point where we are experiencing fears that often are not harmful at all. For example, standing up in front of a crowd and giving a speech is not life-threatening or dangerous. However, your brain may perceive it as being so and as a result, may generate feelings of fear. When you feel these fears, your brain is virtually always trying to protect you from something. It is as simple as that. As you experience fears in your life, all you need to do is acknowledge that your brain is trying to protect you from doing something dangerous and then take back control by manually navigating your way through that scary situation. This way, you can override the biological reaction of "something bad is going to happen" and act in spite of that, allowing you to achieve the results you desire to achieve.

How To Reframe Your Fears

The best way to get through your fears is to reframe them. Reframing your fears ultimately means that you acknowledge your fear is there in an effort to protect you from a perceived danger and then finding a new way to see the trigger of your fear. For example, let's say you are afraid of going to the gym. If you were to analyze that fear, you might find that your fear stems from people looking at you funny and thinking you are weak or weird. In this case, your fear is not necessarily of the gym but of the people in it who might think you are weak and weird. While this is certainly an uncomfortable fear to have, it is not one that is ultimately going to lead to you being put in harm's way or exposed to a dangerous situation. Rather than succumbing to the fear, then you could choose to reframe it.

To reframe your fear, you will start by acknowledging exactly *why* you are afraid. Then, you will begin to look for ways to debunk the extent of the fear or ultimately determine that while the fear might be scary, it is not life-threatening. Even if the fear were to come true, you would continue to live on and would likely continue to have a thriving life afterward, which means it is not as urgent or impactful as your brain might have you believe. With this minimization process done, you can move on to finding something new and more positive to think about the scary situation. For example, "Yes, the people at the gym might think I am weak and weird, but I am choosing to be proud of myself for committing to showing up and getting stronger every single day." This type of reframe acknowledges that the fear exists, but also acknowledges that there is a positive alternative to the fear that you are facing. All you have to do after this is commit to the more positive alternative and allow yourself to begin to trust in yourself and your ability to see that scary situation through no matter what. Through this, you will find yourself experiencing a much higher quality of life as you continually smash through your fears and create the results you desire no matter what might attempt to stand in your way.

Developing the Confidence To Succeed

Aside from overcoming fears, another thing you can try to do is develop the confidence that you need to succeed. A great way to do this is to develop a fear-busting method that you use to proactively overcome fears and keep yourself in a state of positive energy as you go. This might include doing anything from dressing in a way that makes you feel confident in adopting a way of speaking to yourself that helps you feel confident. It can also help to have a method that you consistently use whenever you face a fear in your life so that you can reinforce that method and grow to trust in it as being an effective and sustainable method for overcoming your fears.

The more you work with your mentor, the more you will likely find that confidence is something we develop over time and not something we are born with. In fact, your mentor may just have a "confidence method" that they can teach you to help you become more confident in your life. As you begin to learn about this method, again, make sure that you apply it exactly as you are taught it so that you can begin to effectively make these changes and experience the results you are looking for in your life.

The more consistently you work toward building your confidence muscle in life, the easier it will be for you to overcome your fears and act in spite of them. Through this, you will find yourself beginning to move through any obstacle that may rest in your path as you find that they no longer feel scary enough to push you into a state of inaction. This is around the time that most people stop using excuses and start effectively implementing changes in their lives so that they can achieve even more in the long run.

Chapter 14

Dream It Vividly Every Day

The last practice you need to acquire as a part of your success method right from day one is the practice of visualization. Visualization is one of the most powerful tools you will likely ever get your hands on, and it will support you in bringing forward every single dream you have so that you can experience that dream in your reality. In fact, it has been scientifically proven that those who enlist the power of visualization in their personal development skills achieve what they desire much faster and more consistently than anyone else because of how powerful this method is. Using it in your own climb to success and happiness in life is bound to offer you the same results if you use it consistently enough.

The Value Of Visualization

Your mind is the single most powerful tool you have in your life, and yet most people do not know how to use theirs to their benefit. It is easy to receive and follow instructions in the physical sense, but actually getting your mind on board and making consistent changes from a mental point of view can be challenging. Still, if you cannot get your mind on board with changes you want to make or experiences you want to have, you will always struggle with creating the results that you desire to create in your life.

Visualization is a powerful tool because it is the number one tool you can use to condition your mind so that your mindset gets on board with the changes and results you are trying to create. When you use visualization, you begin to overcome many of the mental setbacks that prevent you from achieving success, which, for most people, are the only setbacks that ever hold them back in their entire lives. Visualization can help you overcome fear, low self-confidence and low self-esteem, limiting beliefs that hold you back, and lies that you have told yourself or allowed yourself to believe over the years. As well, visualization can condition your mind to start seeing certain beliefs you desire to have as being true or certain experiences you desire to have as being possible, which allows you to begin to get ready for the things you truly want to have happen in life.

The power of visualization has been proven countless times in life and has been used by everyone from high powered business owners to high-performance athletes for years as a necessary method for success. The reason why it works is because visualization powers certain neurons and neural activity within your brain that leads your brain to believe that your visualized experiences are real. For example, if you visualize yourself speaking in front of a crowd, your brain will believe that is really happening because it has no reason to believe otherwise. It genuinely behaves as if that is real by producing the same thoughts, feelings, and physical experiences that are actually speaking in front of a crowd would produce. If you can use this tool frequently enough, however, you can create circumstances within yourself that allow you to actually become used to the idea of public speaking and even develop certain skills that make it easier. It all starts in visualization and then can be carried over into your actual real life when you sit down and start engaging in that visualized behavior in the real world.

How You Can Turn Your Goal Into a Visualization Practice

Turning your goals and dreams into a visualization practice is easy, but you want to make sure you do it properly so that you are truly aligning yourself for success. You can start by first making sure that you are incredibly clear on exactly what it is that you want to achieve in your life and what you want that to look like. Make sure you have taken the time to get clear on your specifics and that you know exactly how you want to look, feel, and experience those particular goals and results in your life. After you have gotten clear, you want to take time to turn those goals into an actual visualization experience.

To turn your goals into an actual visualization experience, you want to sit back and close your eyes and use your imagination to act as if you are having a memory of you already achieving that particular goal. In order to really make it feel like a memory, you want to do your best to incorporate as many realistic layers into your memory as you possibly can. This means you want to think about what you would see, what you would feel, what you would hear, what you would touch, what you would smell, what you would taste, and what you would notice. You want to do your best to visualize the end result in your mind and then try to interact with that visualization as if you were experiencing it in real life. After all, if it were a memory, it would not just be a static image but something you had actually interacted with in real life.

The more you can bring your visualization to life in your mind through including the senses and attempting to mentally interact with it; the more real your visualization is going to support you with actually bringing that visualization to life. From there, you can use your visualization in whatever way you see fit. This means you can use it to inspire you, to encourage you, to support you with developing new habits, or to otherwise help you create the results you desire to create in your life. Do not be afraid to use this visualization and the tools surrounding it to create whatever you need for yourself so that you can enjoy the life you truly want to enjoy.

Turning Your Visualization Practice Into a Daily Habit

In order to visualization to have its biggest impact and for you to receive the exact results you are looking for, you need to be willing to turn that visualization practice into a daily habit that you do on a routine basis. The more you can incorporate visualization into your daily practice, the more consistently you will use it, and therefore the more it will be able to help you create the results you desire to create. Studies have shown that people who use the power of visualization for even ten minutes per day can massively increase their capacity to create the results they desire to create. This means that if you continue to visualize for just ten minutes per day on your chosen visualization, you will become much more likely to turn that visualization into your real life. If you were to go so far as to even double that visualization time and spend twenty minutes per day visualization, you would likely have even faster and more lasting success with your practice.

In order to really turn your visualization practice into a consistent part of your daily routine, I highly encourage you to make sure that this is a practice that is easy for you and that you look forward to. You can do this by using many tools to help you further improve the way you experience visualization so that it is even more invigorating and successful.

One of the biggest things you can do to improve your visualization experience is beginning to make that experience something that is incredibly peaceful and relaxing. Most of us do not have a strong relaxation routine in place and, as a result, we find ourselves experiencing massive and consistent amounts of stress on a regular basis. By turning your visualization experience into something that is both relaxing and productive, you increase your likelihood of completing it while also making it an even more enjoyable experience. As a result, you begin to develop positive associations with your visualization experience which makes the process even more powerful.

Some of the ways you can start to make your experience even more relaxing and powerful is through listening to meditation music as you visualize, lighting candles or burning incense, or even diffusing essential oils, sitting or lying somewhere comfortable, and wearing comfortable and loose clothes as you visualize. There are plenty of things you can do to make the experience even more relaxing, so do not be afraid to personalize that part of your experience. You could even practice visualization from the tub or while in your bed at night right before you fall asleep or first thing when you wake up in the morning.

Aside from picking the most relaxing experience to go along with your meditation, you might also wish to incorporate other elements that make it even easier. Some people will use a recorded visualization as a way to help themselves stay focused and really sink into visualization rather than spending the time getting distracted and overwhelmed by those distractions. If you cannot find a guided visualization meditation track on YouTube that gives you the exact experience you want to have, you might consider having someone make one for you so that you get the exact experience you are looking for. It can be quite simple to make one yourself, as well if you find that you have an easy time listening and relaxing to your own voice.

Once you have made the entire experience relaxing and more enjoyable, the last thing you need to do is make it consistent and hold yourself accountable. Make sure that you schedule time for visualization every single day, and that you do it every single day. Even just those ten minutes before you fall asleep can really have a huge impact on your ability to create more of what you want in your life, so do not be afraid to do what you can to incorporate it into your schedule.

Some people do find that using motivational practices like a reward system or having an accountability partner when it comes to visualization can be incredibly helpful in keeping them on track. They may find that by putting a sticker on a calendar, ending the experience with something like a delicious breakfast, lunch, or dinner, or otherwise making the experience even more rewarding, they are more likely to stick to it. Sometimes, these forms of instant gratification are necessary to hold you over as you work toward the results you desire, so do not be afraid to do whatever you need to do to keep yourself on track.

Conclusion

Creating change in your life is no easy feat; that is why many people never successfully change. Often, people find themselves lusting after what life *could* be like and dreaming about how things *could* be "if only." Or, worse, they find themselves no longer dreaming because they are afraid to own up to the fact that those dreams may never come true because they are largely unwilling to do what it takes to make those dreams come true.

You have successfully read this book, which means that I know you are ready to create serious change in your life, and you are ready to have your dreams become your reality. You are no longer interested in sitting around creating excuses; you want to experience the real deal. The fact that you have committed yourself to reading everything within this book just proves that you are ready to stop being the type of person who only hears what needs to happen and to start being the type of person who actually makes it happen. But I have to remind you; change does not happen from knowing what needs to take place; it happens from action. After you read this book, you might find yourself lingering in a state of complacency as you wrongfully believe that knowing the knowledge contained within this book is enough to make a difference. The reality is: it is not.

If you take what you have learned here and hold onto it, never actually acting on what you have learned, you are guaranteed to never get anywhere beyond where you are right now. At that point, the only reason you have learned this book is to satisfy yourself and to have the opportunity to say "you tried" even though, at that point, you and I would both know that you truly did not give that try your effort. In life, the "college effort" is not strong enough to create the results you desire. If you want to have serious changes in your life, you need to go out there and make serious changes happen so that you can start enjoying everything life has to offer.

I know you have what it takes to actually implement what you have learned in this book and to take action on everything your mentor has told you. I know that within your heart, there is a fire burning that has you wanting so much more than just an excuse to say you tried. You *want* serious change. You want to overcome that complacency and procrastination within yourself that you have been experiencing that continually holds you back. You want *more*. And now you have exactly what it takes to make more happen in your life.

Right now, if you have not already, it is time for you to find yourself a mentor. Take the goals you have set for yourself and the dream you have made for yourself and start looking for someone who can seriously get you toward where you want to go in life. Make sure you find someone who really resonates with you, then start learning all there is to know from that person. Pay attention to how they speak, think, and behave. Ask them what you can to find out more about how you can start making the necessary changes they have made to experience the same results in your life. Do not be afraid to do everything you can to educate yourself on their method for success so that you can implement that same method and become successful in your own life, too.

And, for the love of all things good in this world, *do not try to do it your own way*. The wheel spins because it is round. The method works because it was made to. When you are learning and just beginning to create the results you desire is not the time to start improvising and trying to mastermind your way into the results you desire. Right now is the time to be the student, to listen, and to show up applying the methods you have been taught to create the results you want to create.

Following those methods you learn is not for the faint of heart, and not everyone will have the bravery and courage required to see those methods through. But if you are willing to stay the course and keep trying, and if you have chosen the right mentor, I can guarantee you are going to see the results you desire to see in your life.

If you have gotten this far and you feel like *I Heard You: How To Achieve What You Want, and Live Happy* has supported you in finally stepping beyond procrastination and excuses and into changes and results, I ask that you, please take a moment to review it on Amazon Kindle. Your honest feedback on this book would be greatly appreciated as it will help me create even more great titles to help you achieve the results you desire in your life.

Thank you, and do not forget to stock up on notebooks and pens! You have a lot of notes to take and a lot of studying to do. You can do it!

Printed by Amazon Italia Logistica S.r.l.
Torrazza Piemonte (TO), Italy